AN I

"I am in love with Amelie and the sweet honeysuckle energy and taste she radiates through her words, onto my own tongue. Learn and love what she has to say, you will never regret it. So fucking gorgeous. Tender, sweet, and raw, she shares the fruit that embodies our lives. This poetry book is something to treasure and not read over once. It is a lifetime of feelings to last forever, encapsulated in paper."
- Kendall Hope, Author of *Pockets of Lavender*

"*What Once Was An Inside Out Rainbow* is a beautiful journey of self and nature, bursting with gorgeous imagery and ripe food for thought. Amelie creates scapes, not just with the words she writes, but also with the unique way that she arranges them."
- John Queor, Author of *Resembling A Moth*

"A lovely collection focusing on the many aspects of love, disappointment, and finding one's footing through it all. With flower-filled and art gallery imagery, this collection will walk you through the feelings so many of us face when dealing with the mundane and the extraordinary aspects of life."
- Tiffiny Rose Allen, Author of *At The Beginning Of Yesterday*

"*What Once Was An Inside Out Rainbow* is an amazing debut following a stream-of-consciousness style of poetry. It is vulnerable. It is beautiful. It is simply art. I can't wait to see what else Amelie Honeysuckle has for us."
- Flor Ana, Author of *A Moth Fell In Love With The Moon*

"Amelie Honeysuckle uses her words so beautifully to paint the picture of her life as artwork and how life can be messy, confusing, exciting, and invigorating all at the same time, becoming aware of the intimate relationship we can have with nature and finding solitude in the beauty that exists within us and around us."
- Courtni A. Tansey, Author of *Ready to Evolve*

WHAT ONCE WAS AN INSIDE OUT RAINBOW

A POETRY COLLECTION

AMELIE HONEYSUCKLE

Cover Art Copyright © 2023 by Amelie Honeysuckle
Illustration Copyright © 2023 by Amelie Honeysuckle

Edited by Flor Ana Mireles

1st Edition | 01
Paperback ISBN: 979-8-9862106-4-3

First Published April 2023

For inquiries and bulk orders, please email:
indieearthpublishinghouse@gmail.com

Printed in the United States

1 2 3 4 5 6 7 8 9

Indie Earth Publishing Inc.
| Miami, FL |

INDIE EARTH
PUBLISHING

WHAT ONCE WAS AN INSIDE OUT RAINBOW

Amelie Honeysuckle

TABLE OF CONTENTS

For Kendall, Arianna, JiaMiao, Rin, Madeline, Miles, Anna, Colin, Grant, Luke S., Luke B.

The ability to create art in a flow state can speak to many and help those who don't understand finally get it.

Let each word consume you as you construct your own interpretation of the poetry inside...

ART GALLERY GRAND OPENING

I will give you everything,
do my best to show you everything,
all that I am,
because I deserve to show you.
You are not obliged to listen
or to watch
or to hear,
but I will give you everything,
do my best to show you everything,
all that I am,
because I deserve to show you
my body
of beauty,
laced in flowers,
honeysuckle vines tickling my fingertips
all
the
way
down
to my toes.
You are not obliged to listen
or to watch
or to hear,
but I will give you
my sunsets,
my sunrises,
my mountain ridge lines.
Words I define by
the colors I lace myself in,
a soul I nourish with magical medicine,
aspirations I am creating.
I am the fucking art gallery,
and I will give you everything,

do my best to show you everything
all that I am,
because I deserve to show you.
You are not obliged to listen
or to watch
or to hear,
but I will give you everything,
do my best to show you everything
all that I am.
Welcome to the grand opening of my art gallery.

It Begins

Sick stomach,
wooziness,
stars glimmering.
I just waved goodbye
at the intersection
to the one yesterday.
Who let me do this?
Oh, that's right, I did.

Fascination

To love a part of the world,
of reality around you,
and to be drawn to it,
so easily amazed,
and you assume everyone
feels the same,
but really,
it is just you
and the feeling
uniquely yours
as you sit
mesmerized by the mountain rocks
or by the clouds.

*We all have one thing
we think everyone else
is just as marveled by
as we are.*

The White Hat & Brown Hair Glare

To see your lover,
for him to not be your lover,

                              but 600 miles away,

missing your lover.

To hope
that, one day,
you see your lover
where you thought you saw
your lover
today.

Shade in the Middle of the Day

One journal and a pen,
two kids throwing a ball,
couples soaking in the shade after a hike,
old people with sticks,
young people reading,
smooth life,
butterfly
soaring,
"Look it's a butterfly!"
young life,
unaware of where they are.
Shoes off,
comforted by the shade of
the big tree in the middle.

Do Not Ask, Just Know

You cannot ask a tree to grow
too many
or
too little leaves.
We cannot ask our tree to stop being a tree.
We cannot ask our tree to shade this part of the yard
more than that side.
We cannot ask our tree to stop growing
as it rains.
We cannot ask our tree
because the tree
simply is.

She's a Good Actor

I need you
and I know you know.
You're aware,
but I asked
the other night
and the only thing that looked back at me
was a ridge line
and some stars.
So, I'll figure it out
and not say such things.

A mom who hasn't seen her children
in five years
tells her on her first day
she misses them.
She lost custody
so, she's here?
Now?

A mom—
not really a mom—
a vessel only to him.
A little crazy, I assume.
Alone now.

A mom, not to me.
It's been ten years,
she's no mom to me,
but alone
and drives me crazy,
"Please leave."

Just go,

but to know
she's out there,
but not the idea you would hope
her to be as she
has left me feeling like all the stars have imploded on me.
So, exist in the ridgeline
and the stars looking back at me.

Feathered Friend

I read
and I look up to see
a bird at my toes
under me.
I rock back and forth
using the tiny muscles
in my feet
to push me
as I read and look up to see
a bird hopping
beneath me,
from one side of
the chair
to the other.
Hop!
It's on the rocking chair
to my right.
Hop!
One more over.
He crooks his neck,
we make eye contact.
Hop!
One chair
to the left.
Hop!
He's back under me.
I do not rock,
I sit and smile.

Awareness

I have been told,
as advice,
to have no expectations
but to enjoy life,
let the fear go,
for violence is
only created by
someone trying to
mold the gold
in you,
to "guide" you,
but when
you have no expectations,
by others or yourself,
you exist.
Others lose control
because
"I'm an ass, you're an ass."
Others lose control
when you simply enjoy one's company,
but do not need their company
you can be alone
and enjoy your book,
a sunset,
the flowers.
No expectation
and there will be no fear
in you.
Therefore, no violence.
Awareness
of no expectations, control, external reality, emotions inside of you, that
are not you, flowers, thunder, biking, smiling, things, jewelry, conversa-
tions, time, trees, leaves, tattoos, water, ground, rocks, coloring,

creation, learning, walking, sleep, love.
Love will be awake
in you, not *with you*, but in you.
Release, let go, but do not
try to or it will be temporary.
It is beautiful
and I'm barely there,
but I have been told,
as advice,
to have no expectations
but to enjoy life.

Isn't that beautiful?

Union

A son
and dad,
throwing ball
on the lawn
by the big tree.
He could be about
21
Or 16.
Who knows?
Who cares?
He's older,
probably has gray hair.
Smack!
Toss!
From one glove
to another.
They chase the ball
when he doesn't catch it.
They made sure to bring
the gloves
and ball
with them.
He said, "Do not forget the gloves and ball, it is important."
And here they are now,
throwing ball
on the lawn
by the big tree
just before bed.
Life's simplicities.

Green Magic for Me

Where the magic flows,
a secret oasis.
A waterfall of crystals.
Green forest
creating a blanket
where those who
just so happen to be,
lucky enough to see,
another entering or exiting.
The blanket of green
that keeps such magic
a secret
may experience the
sounds and sights
of where the magic flows.

Healing Means Mending, Not Fixing

Time to oneself,
no one present,
no one near,
simply alone.

> Breathe freely,
> watch openly,
> kiss the sky,
> hold yourself,
> be with yourself.

> It may be all you need,
> I pinky promise.

Flattery

Seeking adventure,
the way life moves
when you barely move.
Sitting in a field of green,
the world tickling your toes.
"This one is a big piggy."

Seeking slow moving time,
fresh air so blue.
Nothing can glue you down,
sitting in your brown rocking chair
in a field of Earth,
sprinkles of colors circle you,
reminding you to...

Seeking independence,
how life vibrates through your core
when you are alone
in your meadow of untouched life,
crying out
for the beauty of time.

Seeking translucent nature,
kissing the trees as you walk past,
thanking them for their time
on this Earth,
gifting the flowers, the flattery
of consuming their fragrance,
counting each blade of grass
and all the sticks hidden
between each blade,
spinning in circles,
smooching the air,

smiling to yourself as you
remember why you're here.

Thankful for the chance to seek
adventure,
all the pleasure to find all
adventures translucent,
for if she sings to you in your
body, almost unwillingly, then she
is your adventure to have
and you ought to seek more
all while you can.

Amelie Honeysuckle

Reality to Longing

What once was
beautiful,
no longer in front of our eyes,
sitting many miles away,
awaiting.

What once was
growing,
no longer in front of our eyes.
"Alone," maybe, but free.

What once was
my life,
now no longer
in a room that really is mine,
working for an end
that isn't
defined.

What once was
new experiences,
now old and just stories,
consuming the time before
what once was.
No longer serving me
because I have taken the time
to see.

What once was—oh the beauty that was in front of me.

Nonsense

I write for you,
for I enjoy nothing more than you.

Sing to yourself
silly things.

Something calling?
Or are your ears ringing?

Alone, but with your own
kissing on the phone.

Hold yourself,
see who you are,

but breathe.
Who are we?

Hey, hey, my baby,
miss me.

You say,

"Stay away."

I wish
to eat with you today

the best piece of art
in my art show.

I create,
but I think,
"My art cannot take me anywhere."

Amelie Honeysuckle

                                                              Why not?
                              I cry to know how this
                              magic simply flows.

Why can't I be alone
but carry you with me?

                              Who are you supposed to be to me?
                                                      Marry me?

I seek myself,
but can act ugly,
but try, aren't we all the same?

I wish to kiss you goodnight,
make no sense,

                                                              shut up,

love me,

                                                                   stop.

To create art,
by me,
for me,
explore, don't
consume.

DO NOT CONSUME.
                                              You are consuming...

Goddamn it.

                                                          Try again.
                                                  Stop rethinking.

Think and let it pass.
It is time to
marry me?

Who cares?
Fuck off,

run around,
almost drown and

do it again,

but kiss me goodnight

before you go
and tell me,

"Marry me."

Good one.

Now try again.

Run on dirt,
up and down
and fall down.

Bleed blood,
obviously.
What else?

Giggle.
You're bleeding!

Yes!

I can bleed!
The rocks have my blood on them!
Yay!
I can bleed!

Now get up
and finish your run.

On trail,
off.

Sleep.
You're healed.
Remind yourself
that
you
can
bleed.
Smile! Be happy!

                                        Shut up, it hurts.

Kiss my neck,
rub my legs,
look at me,
I love you,
brown tint, green look.

You are here
and I know.

                                        Hey, hey, my, mine,

spin with me.

                                                Get dizzy!
                    Get dizzy, dizzy, dizzy.

Remember the day of the week?
Me either
                    BECAUSE WE ARE DIZZY
Giggle, go slow.
Yes, oh, wow.
Kiss me.
Nerves.
Wow and would you look at that,
                    time to go?!
                                        Yup, have to be there at 3.
Shut up.

Lullaby

Sing to me
like you are in love with me.

Sing to me
like we are dancing on a checkerboard
floor,
black and white.

Sing to me like you
are going to take my hand
and spin me
in circles.

Sing to me
like you're leaving this place with me.
To the cosmos
and back,
to another lifetime
but with me.

Sing to me like
this song is ours,
but *make* it ours.

Sing to me like you know,
like you know know what
I'm thinking already.
Undo my clothes,
engrave yourself in me,
trace my perimeter.

Sing to me
like I have been singing to you.

I hope you see
you are the red sand to my red rock.

Sing to me
as we dance in the rain,
into the mist.
Pitch a tent,
we're sleeping wherever we want tonight
like you are in love with me.

Magical Consumption

She ate alone
until it *ate* her,
but with pleasure,
she lets it consume her.

"Hey, I still feel sober."

"Me too, I'm nauseous."

Damn.

They wait,
they color their world
how they see it now.

Sunsets pleasurably warm,
glistening.
Music makes her vision
seem different.

The colors in the blanket,
of black,
now potent.

The clouds in the sky
mold for her,
glistening,
shining for *you*.

I've been in love before.
I know what it feels like.

A woman sharing smoke
with a man,
heavy breasted.

Amelie Honeysuckle

Faces on a melting
rock.

"Have these colors always
been this beautiful
and we've just
never
noticed?"

A nod.

Wow.

A greater awareness of life.
Two black figures
dancing.
I bet they know how to love.
I'm in love
and I love you.

HEAR ME,
beautiful man,
not so beautiful man,
family is everything.
Stay calm, let moments
pass.
Consume me please.

Toddler Tendencies

Lakes of rainbows,
as they call.
Water,
fall on me,
kiss my eyebrow.

Walk,
as they fall.
Water,
fall on my lover,
kiss him with your nectar.

Ponder,
as I speak to the fern—*I promise it moves*—feels silly, but I know you're
alive.
Water,
fall on us,
kiss our connection.

Hey, babe,
sit and play.

Another day.
Are we broken?
OR OKAY?

WE ARE OKAY.
Yay.

A moose?
Can't believe we almost
didn't come.

Amelie Honeysuckle

Tent up,
can of beans.

Another day,
fog on you.

Lay on me,
stare at me.

Okay, that's
too much.

What are we
doing here?

Rain and you and me
and our rain.

I find this is
living,

what I've been
missing.

 $19—plus the funds
spent on
the adventure not had.

Rainbow lakes
kiss me,
fall into me,
vivid memory.

hold eye contact,
fuck me,
dance in me,

vivid memory.

Drunk on
rainbow lakes
of fog
rainfall
falls on.

Rainbow electric
nature,
dirt in my toenails,
fuck me
tomorrow in
my vivid memory.

Stare at yourself,
in me, ponder.
Now, this is living.

Fake Allergies

She was allergic to honey.

He said, "Okay,
no more."

Then, he left,
and she cried.

She was allergic to honey.

He said, "Okay,
marry me?"

Then, she married him,
able to confide.

Self-Explanatory

To encapsulate you
in a few words:
Impossible.

When It Rains

Worn brown brimmed hat.
Mauve dress to wrinkled knees.

Gray hair,
not yet balding...
One of the lucky ones.

Strum my guitar,
crack my back,
fold me in two.

By bike,
we could travel.

By van,
we could experience

salty face—
that's sweat—
crunch of rock
in our bear paws,

imprinting by cause,
stuck here in education.
—Pause—

The skyline
completed one time
would complete another
time
over,
worth more than
any goddamn

dime.

Spinning chair,
we kiss,
first time,
pushing away from you,
lost control.
Pick me up,
dip me down,
dirty dancing
to town.
In one second,
it was all ours.
Forever in love,
this I know
in a dream.

Live well,
the goodness he gave me.
The future is bright.
Bought what you sold,
best decision I ever made.

Strum your guitar for me,
crack my code
ever so slow now.

The freedom I've been,
It's something of feeling.
You're wonderfully breathing.
Blessed in the rainfall,
we're cleaned in the downpour.

Be safe.
Be true.
Best believe I'm forever with you.

Never save me
from his goodness.

He's like a morning:
Fresh.
New.
Awaiting.

Live well.
Dressed finely.
Dapper.

I'll see you soon
in the rainfall.

Adopted Salvation

Laced in colors,
she sparkled
when spoken to,

but when forced
to speak,
all thoughts
vanished.

Seen in black and white,
she the most detailed.

"Hello, mom, why must you..."
Red, yellow, green, blue...

"Well, honey, you see..."
Gray and purple...

"But, mommy! I don't want to!"
Orange, violet, navy...

"I don't care! Grab your shit and go!"
Ugly, transparent, nonexistent...

She cries and walks
down away,

but losing her colors,
becoming black and white.

She lost a mom
and her colors

until one day
"Happy anniversary! Ma!"

A figure, strong, passionate
"Can you trim my hair?"

Ma, mama,
a gift, a rescue.
She saved her, helped
replenish
the colors
lost—

Not all, that's impossible,
but some.

Red, pink, blue,
she gained a new one.
Thanks, ma.

Forced to Work

Are you afraid of me?

Do I scare you?

Boo!

Or am I afraid of you?

You do scare me?

Or are you just insecure?

You're afraid?

What happens when
we're afraid
of one another?

We both can't be scared.

Boo!

Good one, real funny.
Now,
what am I to do?

Speak to me like
that again
and I will curse you
in my head
and take your scared,
abuse-
confusing sheman.

Now, fuck you, let's be
friends.

Blissful Peach Tree

A woman so loving,
a hug,
open arms
upon first encounter.

She's beautiful.
I see where he gets it from.
Love pouring out of her,
kisses on one's shoulder.

How does one learn to love
as deeply as she?

How does one carry herself
as elegantly as she?

So intriguing,
she knows so much.
So intelligent,
so experienced
and such.

Easy to love,
easy to die for.
I admire you
and all that you could
cry for.

A woman so grand,
she defines her title
more than any "idol."

Easy to love,

loving is she,
open arms
always she greets me.

Well, hello!
I absolutely love
speaking with you,
beautiful nature.

A blissful peach tree
she ought to be,
always sharing her
fruit
with many more
than just me,
obviously.

Nectar so sweet,
let it drip down your cheek.
Don't you dare wipe your feet.
Sit and just be
with her
as she models being free in one's mind.

You can't help but
crave more,
beautifully crafted
woman,
never so poor.

So glad we meet,
a peach tree so
profound,
deep, deep roots in the ground.
Oh, how lucky I was to have found
your baby peach tree

as he has led you to me,
me to you
more like it.

Make many others
loosen their crown
as it belongs to
Mother Earth,

The woman of
all, many hours,
wise peach tree
she ought to be.
Oh, I am so glad
you welcome me
with the hug,
open arms
upon first encounter.
I aspire to be like you,
elegant peach tree.

She Taught Me to Look at the Sky

An inspiration for my writing,
you set over the horizon,
but not the setting sun,
circumpolar,
all the time,
never set,
always there,
smiling high,
working on oneself,
living to live
and not to die,
only sometimes,
oh my.

Where will you go,
my dear?
Who are we?
Old?
Certainly not?
Want some magic?
Consume some
with me
as we did
that one time
when left alone,
river bright,
melting sky.

We are doing just fine.
Thank you geysers
for imploding,

as it lead me to you,

this I am sure.
A big sister,
I am so grateful
for us and who we are.

Thank the clouds.
They follow you
and you to the sky,
taught me the beauty
and such secured
in the inside out
of all rainbows
ever seen,

the most magical one
seen with you
and that's how I knew
I knew you before.
Thank you.
Will always be here for you,
the inside out rainbow
made sure I knew.

Fragile Essence

Columbine,
way too fine,
hide your secrets,
as you hide your time.

Work to no expense,
expend your secrets,
just as you have mine.

Exist to be
and be to exist
while you are working
to be existent all the time.

Valuable in
relationship,
for our bond has no price.
I wish to see you
beyond the star line,

loving, coexisting,
but with time
to explore your mind,
is to implore all kind.

A beauty so strong,
so insanely fine.
I ask you always
"What's on your mind?"

Lip locked and luscious,
I know you cry
a soul of a thousand

gooey clouded sunsets.
You know why.

Who will you be
when given the time?
You are gorgeous,
a juicy grape vine,

turned into wine.
When drank just right,
flavor so intense,
your fruit hits just right.

And when we're woozy,
thanks to your grape vine,
we will dance under
your gooey sky,

care for all as you
are incapable of
caring for none.

We indulge you
with no stop
to get woozily stunned.

Summit

A waterfall that cannot flow...
It simply cannot know...
Uh oh.
Soon,
when rocks tumble onto
where she sprinkles
slow.

Ouch.
Does it hurt?
Good, now it is time to know.
Push your water.
Go.

Drip by drip from
the peak above.
How tall do you shove?
Up

down and around,
rushing water sounds
hitting the ground.
Now she knows.
Good to go.

Revelations

I need you in order to get around.
Up from the ground,
we levitate
as we build this
newly found
euphoria

onto our similarities,
profound,
but barely found
and mostly underground.

A lovely harmony,
we love,
one we thought would
never be found.

Experiences are
all we needed
in order to
bend one
leg up from
such silly ground.

We know
and have learned
what it means.
So, now we love
in harmony,
excited for experience,
love built on needing
each other to get around.

I never want to
wallow in that ground,
for we love in
such precision
encouragement,
in exploration.

I want to see you flourish,
expand,
grow,
develop,
but know
I will never let go
and am so excited to
see you go around.

Quietly Loud Wishing for You to Hear Me

Do you know that you are loud?
I cannot speak.
I CANNOT SPEAK!

Do you know you pretend to be emotionally available
but hide when approached with the chance
to actually feel emotions?

I CANNOT SPEAK
when you yell over me!
Who am I to think?

Perhaps I should continue to NOT SPEAK
because that makes sense,
you "emotionally available" man.

Do you know that I am trying to talk?
Or is it more fun
to hear yourself speak words
when I cannot
I CANNOT SPEAK?

I'll sit here and munch on my sandwich
while you speak nonsense,
because who am I to try and speak.

Bluegrass Fun

Lips raw,
I want to know you all,
I find you so perfect.

You care out of concern,
always aware,
never dare,
except that one time,
but that was not fair.

Kiss me, my love,
tambourine my knee,
give me you,
it's all you do.

Indeed, it is true,
I need nothing more than you.
The journey of us
is one I cannot wait for.
Give me you!

I find you so perfect,
dirty birdy.
Attentive
until you are not,
but your face
was down and dirty.
She hurt.

Knees raw,
pleading for you,
never wheel away.
Do not crunch my

vertebrae.

I find you so perfect,
built so exact,
it made me know,
no more passing through,
only alone together.

Tambourine my thumb.
We're here to summit
until our lips are raw
and cannot thaw.

Broken Love

Why do they not look
back
at each other
after kissing
and turning backs?

Amelie Honeysuckle

Genera of Living

My hips move in a forward movement,
spinning next to me.
My ankles rotate,
cartilage cracking
from my poor structure.

The sound of the sky,
beautiful day,
the air I am able to breathe,
the beauty of living.

Existing does not have to be complex.
Spend any time,
any at all,
that you get
today
just being.

Remember the simplicities
like rolling through the sky,
two wheels on the ground,
legs in circular motion
towards a place
you call home
with your best friends inside
ready to ask you about your day.

Remember music
and how easy it is to let your body giggle,
wiggle your arms—is that
a twinkle in your eye I see?

Put some thought into your outfit,

wear what you want to wear—
colorful or not.
I have a professor that wears nothing but black.

I prefer my colors
and my spinning hips
as I go to and fro
five days a week.
I find the beauty in the air,
the beauty in the sky,
beauty in the twirling clouds,
music in my ears,
body giggling.

I stare at the faces I pass when walking around,
just to look,
look to see,
see to feel,
feel to think,
think to know,
know to enjoy,
enjoy to feel,
feel to think,
think to know.
And now you're back,
the circular motion
I know so well
and damn am I glad I do.

Beautiful day,
banjo singing in my ears,
smile at yourself.

Smell the sky,
zone out as you watch each cloud twirl
for you.

They are twirling for you
because they are happy that you notice them.
While some people put their head down
at their feet
and walk from A to B,
you are looking up.
So, yes, they twirl for you—won't you
twirl for them, too?
Spin for the clouds as a thank you.

Beautiful day,
all you need are a few moments
just enjoy.
Remember that you enjoy to feel.
Do you feel it in your soul?
Awareness is lingering.
Do not try, or it will not work.
Let yourself fall back to where it was when you were a child
and you noticed everything
without knowing you did
because you were new
and the world was vibrant.

Feel to know
and this is when you know.
I promise you will know
as you take a few seconds
to look around
and see all the sounds.
Yes, you can see sounds.
No, I am not crazy.
I am just becoming aware.

Beautiful day,
every day,
feel your world around you

by barely trying to feel it
and there you have it,
knowing of a beautiful day.

Yummy air,
temperature crafted for you,
all on how your nerves interpret the world around them.
Music in your ears,
your brain active,
dancing in your head,
let your body move,
cracks in the pavement
from time and wear.

Beautiful day,
every day,
all you have to do
is look
see,
feel,
enjoy,
think,
know.
Just do not try.

Dripping from My Thumb

Is there honeycomb
in your bones?

Because you taste
so sweet,
there must be.

My love,
oh, my lovely.

Sprinklers

I used to wonder
why I was gifted you.

I actually never wondered
because I already knew.
Twin flame, soul sister, beautiful kisses her.
All I can do is thank you,
because without
that chance to talk to you,

I would have broken a foot
during the most important dance.

Is It Okay If I Write About You?

Waterfall,
lavender,
babe,
my love,
mountain goat,
perfect hue,
green eyes, brown tint,
muscles, too,
intellectual,
blue,
strong, not many knew.

We'll Care for You

Curiosity blooms when I think of you.
Who are you?
I do not really know.
We do not really know,
but we want to.

We ask you,
but you direct our feets
to a different beach.
This sand looks different?
But you tell us it is yours.

Okay, my friend, I guess that is all
we need to know in the end.

Unwarranted Advances

Sadness was in me
because someone else
was in you,
and now you're blue,
but it's too late.
Fuck you.

Giggles

We all always sit
and wonder
where you find your blubber,
and we love it,
could sit in thunder
with you
for hours
and never shudder
because we adore your blubber.

A Love Letter to the Matchmaker

There is a creak of a door
I know no more,
engulfed in darkness,
blind all to the core.

Odor of piss
seeps through your walls,
you nasty bitch,
hope you slip and fall.

To Count on You

Kind and shining,
endlessly blinding,
gifted with conversation,
but no alliteration,
simply pure,
smart with no cure,
until it is found,
deep deep in town,
a secret shop,
I hope it is not,
but it is true,
now that I started sipping on you.

Carefully in Pain

A fire flame
on my window pane.
Her sparks finagle
their ways to each gaggle.
She is flavorful,
the ashes burn.
So precious, so pure.
She worries about you
without you knowing
as she walks around.
Fluffly cloud
catching emotions
that spring back
like a wall ball
into the atmosphere.
A fire flame
circulating on my window pane.

Options

The water that we drink
is what drinks us.
Choose.

Floral

A jacket I love
but have yet to wear
falls off the back of my chair.

Effortlessly Gifted Gold

Walking outside,
the only one awake
or so you think.
No one else is moving,
still air for only you to breathe.
Each step you make is heard,
but by only you, of course.
You could scream so loud,
run around in circles
and it would only be you who hears.
You can go about your business
alone,
completely secluded.
That is the beauty of the morning.
Crisp air rubbing itself up and down your leg,
prickling your nose until you scrunch it up against your face.
You can taste the springtime,
stick out your tongue
and stare at it
until you go cross-eyed.
Laugh at yourself a little,
experience the mindfulness.
You are the morning,
the morning is you.
We are together—
that is the beauty of the morning.

Words You Didn't Know You Knew

Honey dew,
honey do,
honey knew,
honey knew what to do about honey dew.
Apple crisp,
apple kiss,
apple lisp,
apples crisply kiss my lips.

Origin

Concept of getting ready for your day.
Concept of breathing.
Concept of drinking.
Concept of laughing.
Concept of a neighborhood.
Concept of enjoying a moment.
Concept of touching.
Concept of teeter-totters.
Concept of gardening.
Concept of cuddles.
Concept of doing something for the last time.
Concept of sleeping on someone.
Concept of living for the moment.
Concept of being angry.
Concept of being in love with people.
Concept of people living their lives around.
Concept of looking forward to something.
Concept to savoring a moment.
Concept of waking up on your birthday.

Amelie Honeysuckle

Scarf

Orange,
so magnificent,
lined with soft cotton,
almost lace,
bumpy with butterflies of fluff.

Red,
making the swirls that follow
the orange,
adding character.

Brown—
was her color,
so she lent me her discovery,
knowing I'd be better at consuming
such color
than her brown.

I wear her around my neck,
draped over my shoulders.
I smile at myself in the mirror,
seeing the colorful versions
of such orange,
playing with each other,
hanging around me,
adding vibrancy
color to the PJs
orange.

Age

Do you ever look
at what once was
seen in your mirror
and wonder who she is,
who she simply was?
Entangled in a meadow—
Engulfed in honeysuckles and tulips—
drowning in this meadow—

Do you ever look
at what once was
seen in your mirror
looking back at you?
She is you,
prancing around in her meadow,
absolutely downing
by what was done.
So much so,
she tattooed this meadow
onto her
honeysuckle ribs.
She breathes tulips—
sounds beautiful?
But there is a reason why
these flowers
follow her
in their beauty,
because during her run of shit,
they were the most beautiful thing
in her life.
They kept her going,
they gave her that second of
beauty

she so craved
but could barely find
in her own meadow.
So, she tattooed them on her body,
because to her,
they are her.
Because they represent
the most beautiful thing
she saw
and experienced
during her run of shit
and that is why
her meadow has now become a canyon range.
Because after her run of shit,
she went to heal
and that ridgeline
brought her endless beauty
until it was her
and she was it.

To Talk Shit

Why can't we write about the parts
no one wants to?
So sorry you're not a tall sunny, soothing, sexy sunflower,
It fucking rains sometimes
And you suck.
Honestly,
don't we all?
Isn't that why it is okay?
Get a grip, okay.

PCT

There has to be some part of you
                                        that wants to fuck off
                to the middle of nowhere,
where the grass is long
and breezy
and there are trees
that touch the stars,
skim the bottom of satellites.

There has to be some part of you
that wants to see everything
barefoot, dirt in your toenails,
                that wants to walk for miles.
                        How about 2,650 miles, with me?

There has to be some part of you
that wants more.
This is not more.
What we do is not more.
More is nowhere

                                and everywhere all at once.

There HAS to be some part of you
that needs this exploration,
that enjoys wondering,
having no idea where one is to go
and stumbling upon unexpected glory.

There has to be some part of you
that wants to kiss stars unseen,
because you stand under a new vine,
laughing at your toes
as you travel so far

for fun in purity.

There has to be some part of you
that wants to have no idea what tomorrow will hold,
besides eating, sleeping, and moving your body.
THERE HAS TO BE SOME PART OF YOU,
please tune into it, for me, pinky promise, for me.

.

Whitney

Heavy pack,
trail unknown,
cold prone,
walking away from home.

Does your jaw drop
when you realize there are things bigger than you?
How about ones that are jagged
and stand mocking you,
hovering over you?
Tiny little chipmunk,
scream before you can't anymore.

Where will you sleep tonight?
Alone and cold?
Or will you have someone to hold
and still be cold?

To Dad

I love you.
I look at myself
and see you,
and I am glad I am a part of you
and you are a part of me,
because you are a beautiful man
and I know you are my person.

I love you so much.
I am so thankful for all you have taught me
and continue to.
So wise,
so beautiful of a man.
You must know
that you glow
and love us all so much so.

Dad, you make your own happiness.
Obviously, you know,
and you know this is my favorite
key to success
and a happy life,
and I am so grateful for your guidance,
from a beautiful man.

I hope you know
I adore you so,
my inspiration,
my best friend,
the reason why I am everything that I am.
Thank you for being my beautiful man
and holding my hand,
especially when I could barely stand,

my best friend, a beautiful man.

Do You Have Any Questions?

The strangely beautiful woman in the pretty plant shop
said to me, "You don't think
you can make a life out of art,
do you?"
I nodded, agreed.
Then, I turned and made a life out
of fucking artwork.

Functionality

Music shows you how your brain is working,
pay attention to that.
And to others, especially others.

Arched Back, Bent Legs

Do you want to make love
as cherry blossoms fall
from the sky
in between your eyes?

Kiss my hands
and guide them in between your thighs,
look in my eyes,
giggle as we sigh.

Do you want to make love
as golden leaves fall
from the sky
in between your eyes?

Kiss my nose
as you swivel your head
back and forth:
Eskimo kisses.

Do you want to make love
as the snow falls
in between your eyes?

Twirl me in two,
arched back,
cold, but warm enough
because I am with you.

Do you want to make love
as sun rays beam
from the sky
in between your eyes?

Amelie Honeysuckle

Yes?

Yes.

Broken Boundaries

I am an avocado.
How do you wish to slice me open?
Horizontally, vertically, or throw me against the wall?

You want my juices,
but when you bite into me,
I taste like a peach
and you wanted an avocado…
Fuck!

Why are you green?
I wanted purple!
Fuck!

Now, you choose the option of opening me up
by throwing me against the wall…
Interesting,
how unconventional.

And would you look at that?
Perhaps I taste like a peach
because you threw me
against the fucking wall.

It was an option, but quite illogical,
and now I am not what you wanted
and you're saying you've failed me?
Perhaps you are confused, a little distraught.

I taste like a peach because I am one.
I appear purple
simply because I am.
How do you expect to morph me into an avocado?

I must know.

Choking Me Out

You snatched my bundle of tulips
and smacked me across the face with it,
not once,
but twice,
and then went in for the upper cut.

Amelie Honeysuckle

To Exist Only for a Short Verbal Exchange

A crest of red highlights my features while
stopped at a stop light
on my painted bike I've grown to love.

A squeak of a mouse,
or perhaps a shitty bike chain.
Ah, yes, it was a shitty bike chain I heard.

A man pedals through,
we share a quick glance,
my lips move up the right side of my cheek momentarily.

"You are beautiful,"
is said respectfully, and meaningfully.
"Thank you."
"You're welcome."

Then, my red highlights flashed to green.
A quick exchange.
A simple interaction.
But one that left me grinning to myself
all
the
way
home.
How very much that meant to me.
Thank you, man with the shitty bike chain.

Sanctioned Emotion

A tree grips on for life,
digging its roots down deeper.
But they rot from under
him, yet she tugs on.
He calls to the dirt, to
grasp his roots, anything
he can hold.
He crys out,
but no one can save
him, but himself.
Forced to be self reliant,
eager to see her
and create something
a little more free.

He rots away.
A slow death.
One you have to see as you
walk by.
The sun stopped shining
on him.
Leaves refused to grow.
Yet she called out to the dirt,
"Please, hold me?"
The dirt did not reply,
for it is dirt.

The tree began to weep.
The end too near.
Love not found.
Poor tree...
Finally crashing to the ground,
yet this time,

the dirt held him
and rocked him to sleep.
sweet dreams, you poor
rotten tree.

Wanna Play Bikes With Me?

My neck cranks,
hurts a little
as I strain myself to see you
roll around me.
Circles, circles, circles.
Where are you going, baby?

Your neck cranks,
hurts just a little
as you strain yourself to see me
roll around you.
Circles, circles, circles.
Where am I going, baby?

Wherever we go, we will always go together, baby.

There Are Only Beautiful People & Not-so Beautiful People

Have you ever met another
so vibrant
it is almost blinding?

But you don't mind being blind,
instead you embrace it
because you would rather be blind
from having seen another so
beautiful
than to be able to have sight and
see another
not-so
beautiful.

Canyon Ridge Lines Only Rise for Six Weeks a Year

I found a place that was me
just in place form,
not in human form.
I was skeptical at first.
How can this be me?
There is a reason I am here, obviously.

I found a place I could make out with,
and damn, was it a good kisser.

I found a place I morphed with
in a matter of days.
I became it, and it me.
We.

Trails that lead to what may be
all of me.

Sights I imprinted on myself,
energies I collided with
in the correct frequency.
Us.

Who Am I to Judge?

I said I liked your art.
            I lied.

In Terms of Losing Awareness

The birds chirped a lot more
          when you were younger.
                    Ever wonder why that is?

Four Leaf Clover

My grandma found one when she was younger.
I bet she calls herself lucky.
What do you think?

Can luck be determined in a split second,
all at once?
Everlasting love,
float away on me.
Right underneath the biggest tree
while apples fall on me,
and break my toes
as they grow cold.

But hey, I'm lucky,
so apples can fall on me
and break every bone,
tear out my teeth
because to me,
today,
I am lucky.

My Meadow of Wildflowers & Wine

Would you take my hand
and spin me in circles
until I gag,
gasp for air?
In all the time
we spent dancing,
roaming through each blade of grass,
smiling as we make eye contact,
looking in each other's eyes,
our love was hidden under the sky

Sip on me,
just like you do between my thighs,
I'm your dark red wine.
As we gasp for air,
we throw open our lawn chairs
as if we're ever going to take a break and stop dancing.
Like I said,
I'll spin you
round and round until you gag,
gasp for air.
In all the time
we spent dancing,
watching the colors bloom,
all I do is fall for you.
As we sip on our dark red wine,
you are mine.
And I pick for you the best clouds in the sky
as I've created them for you.

I'll Evaporate for You

The best kind of weather
is the one no one likes,
because while everyone is pissing on the sky,
you are looking up
with a smile
saying,
"My, oh my, oh my, what a beautiful sky."

Genuine Questions

Why are there people that take things so seriously?
Why are there people that do not take things seriously?
Why are there people that can score well on exams?
Why are there people that cannot score well on exams?
Why are there people that like vanilla more than chocolate?
Why are there some people that like to scream at kids?
Why are there some people that do not like being cozy?
Why are there some people that are never tired?
Why are there some people that never write?
Why are there some people that prioritize wealth over love?
Why are there some people who have seen every movie?
Why are there some people that hurt others?
Why are there some people that drink more than they should?
Why are there some people that seek approval by others?
Why are there some people that are loud?
Why are there some people that do not try and love?

Manual Reboot

Do you ever act
out of pocket
as you remember that
you are not who you want
and you see that
who you want to be
is too far out of reach?
But who you want to know
you cannot find a way to go,
so you accept defeat
and let your feets
reset to the beat.

Misting

I could just walk away
in the rain
forever.

Let Your Lovers Hold You While You Hurt, Please

If you were swimming in open water
and it seems like there is little hope, you may drown.
But there are people on a boat floating there with you.
They want to help you get out of the water.
It's getting cold.
Would you let them help you?
Or would you turn your back and dive deep down?
As they watch…

If you were shot in the tummy
and it seems like there is little hope, you may bleed out.
But there are people with bandages and wound care.
They want to help stop the bleeding.
You're losing a lot of blood.
Would you let them help you?
Or would you wave these people away and squeeze more blood out?
As they watch…

If you are hurting
and it seems like there is little hope.
But there are people who love you, who would die for you.
They want to help you stop the pain.
The pain is overwhelming.
Would you let these people hold you while you cry?
Or would you choose to isolate?
As you hurt those who love you, while also hurting yourself.

How To Decorate Your Person

How you wear your clothes,
what patterns—
What is in between your nose?

Do your fingers want what no one else knows?
Perhaps you will glow.

In what ways will you show,
THIS IS ME
PLEASE KNOW!

Do you choose basic, or do you choose a show?
Flaunt your shit
because you were pieced together the way that you were
FOR YOU!

How you wear your clothes,
what colors—
What do you wear on your toes?

Does jewelry hang
from your neck?
A flashy show
or delicate
so everyone barely knows.

Dress your person up or down,
but use this as a way to show
and let everyone else know.

If You Have Ears, Use Them

You should probably blare music
L   OU   D!
And then, dance around your kitchen
like no one is
A   ROUN   D!

A Conversation Between a Poppy and a Wisteria

I have heard you've been with them?

Well, I've been busy.

And I choose to go where I wish to go.

As you wish.

Give me a sign.

Of what?

GIVE ME A SIGN!

Why are you yelling?

Give me a sign that you LOVE ME!

What if I do not?

So many questions, so few answers.

No comment.

So short, so little substance.

We are not lovers that share the same nectar.
Who do you think we are then?

Flowers.

Wrong, BEAUTY.

What is your problem?

Questions, questions, questions.

So snappy.

Tell me you love me. I float for you!

You are dramatic.
I am feeling. Perhaps you should feel your emotions sometimes.

Crazy idea.

A Short Comment on Mental Health

Do you take care of plants?
Are they dying?
Check yourself. *Seek help.*

Lady Love

An infatuation,
a lover out of reach.
But, boy, do you crave her scent.
You smell it everywhere
as if her pheromones were created

just
for
you.

An "as you wish,"
whatever she requests.
You will drop to your knees,
bow to her,
She is all you ever need,
all you could desire
and beyond that.
So you do

whatever
she
requests
of
you

A long lost memory:
You've tasted her before
her lips,
barely pure,
drooling as she passes you
with barely a glance.
You need her
and you do not know why.
But, boy, has she done more
than caught your eye.

Amelie Honeysuckle

Soak her up

before
she
says,
"Goodbye."

What World Will You Abide By?

Lay back
and look up,

It's you.

Trying to Hang a Hammock Between Two Charred Trees

Glorification for ugly simplification.
Wash your hands—
they are filthy.
I cannot understand.
When I am with you, I feel like
I am eating sand.
All around, others have
a hammock to swing,
but I stand,
pondering a way to float
between trees, but all I see are broken limbs.
When I need you to, hold me
so I can swing,
but my trees seem to be burning,
charred black
and broken limbs.
Who let you fall apart
and throw me away?
Don't you hear them too?
They are laughing as people like you
hold the hammock,
rock them back and forth,
effortlessly creating a beautiful show.
I kick around mulch
in broken and busted shoes
from walking miles around you,
looking for a new branch to hang on to,
but time is only being
wasted,
drained,
constantly left in pain.
Just call my name.
Act like you even care to explain

who and what allowed
you to bust my candy cane
abrupt and quick,
left kicking mulch
as it rains.
I'd rather drown
in the most beautiful
mountain lake
than wait
and spend one more minute
in this absent pain.

Closing Act - Everything Must Go

We appreciate the time you have spent with us today—
please come again,
especially during the holiday season.
We'll have updated art,
and a two-for-one deal on our ticket entries.
For now,
we hope you've enjoy the show...
We do not get rainbows here often.

SONGS THAT INSPIRED
WHAT ONCE WAS AN INSIDE OUT RAINBOW

What Once Was - Her's

Inside Out - Spoon

Live Well - Palace

Wonderfully Bizarre - Bendigo Fletcher

Blue Ridge June - Sam Burchfield

Lady Love - Thee Sacred Souls

NOTES

The poems *A Conversation Between a Poppy and a Wisteria* and *Lady Love* reference William Goldman's *The Princess Bride*.

When it Rains was inspired and references the song "Live Well" by Palace.

My Meadow of Wildflowers & Wine was inspired and references the song "Wildflowers and Wine" by Marcus King.

The poem *Lady Love* was inspired and references the song "Lady Love" by Thee Sacred Souls.

ACKNOWLEDGMENTS

The book that you are holding only came to be because of Kendall, the endless support of Flor Ana, and the opportunity to purely create with Indie Earth Publishing. I got to watch firsthand Kendall create her debut poetry collection, *Pockets of Lavender*, and was beyond proud of her accomplishments. When I brought up the idea to Kendall of creating my own poetry collection—before I could even finish my sentence—she was telling me to do it. That is love and that is why I want to begin by thanking Kendall Hope for pushing me to create.

My editor, Miss Flor Ana Mireles, and I met almost every Tuesday to work through the process of creating. Flor always greeted me with the biggest smile and gifted endless love and support. Flor acted as one of my top supporters and was always there to hype me up. Thank you Flor for being a magical and grounding person throughout my process of creating.

Indie Earth Publishing gave me a platform to create in a flow state, which is how I write my poetry. I had complete freedom to make sure this poetry book represented me in every way possible. Indie Earth understands how to support authors—experienced or not—and I cannot imagine publishing my book under any other publisher. Thank you Indie Earth Publishing for giving me a platform to share my creation.

The Advanced VIP Readers took time out of their busy schedules to read and review an ARC of *What Once Was An Inside Out Rainbow*. This is no easy task, and each reader did this out of the kindness of their own heart, and, for that, I am forever grateful and appreciate each and every one of you. Thank you, Kendall, John, Tiffiny, Flor, Courtni, Victoria, and Erin for reading my creation.

Arianna, JiaMiao, and Rin were the main people in my life while I crafted most of the poetry in this book. Arianna is my most treasured relationship from my lifetime and I cannot imagine what some of my poetry would be if I did not have her in my life. JiaMiao has a soul that wraps you in a blanket of gold. Rin gave me someone to connect to and was the best person to share new experiences with. I want to thank you three because you helped shape me, whether you knew it at the time or not.

Madeline, Miles, Anna, Colin, Grant, Luke S., and Luke B. are my family and give me endless support. I cannot express to each and every one of you how much I adore you and wake up every morning delighted to have you in my life. You all give me the space to be sensitive and I will always work to be your number one supporter. This book is dedicated to you because I cannot imagine a world without you. Thank you for giving me the space to fall in love with beautiful people and loving me in return.

To the reader, thank you for reading my words. It means everything.

Thank you all for being the reason my art was created.

ABOUT THE AUTHOR

© Madeline Tapp

Amelie Honeysuckle is a student at the University of Colorado Boulder who loves spending her time meandering through her local trails on bike and foot. Amelie is a lover of words and believes that one of the most beautiful ways to colorfully create is through the art of words. She made her literary debut in the poetry anthology *The Spell Jar: Poetry for the Modern Witch*, which released on October 2022. Amelie loves finding unconventional beauty in her environment, thrives through writing love poetry for her people, and is a believer that "you make your own happiness."

Connect with Amelie on Social Media

Instagram: @wordsbyamelie

ABOUT THE PUBLISHER

INDIE EARTH
PUBLISHING

Indie Earth Publishing is an independent,
author-first co-publishing company based in Miami, FL, dedicated to
giving writers the creative freedom they deserve when publishing their
poetry, fiction, and short story collections. Indie Earth provides its
authors a plethora of services meant to aid them in their book publishing
experiences and finally feel they are releasing the book of their dreams.

With Indie Earth Publishing, you are more than just an author, you are
part of the Indie Earth creative family, making a difference one book at a
time.

www.indieearthbooks.com

For inquiries, please email:
indieearthpublishinghouse@gmail.com

Instagram: @indieearthbooks

CPSIA information can be obtained
at www.ICGtesting.com
Printed in the USA
BVHW041303040423
661731BV00008B/480

9 798986 210643